, I found in the heart of a friend lauri

k for happiness outside of ourselves

p; but when thou are in, continue

islike the same things, this is what

w in choosing a friend, slower in

are—that is the poetry in the prose

enough of the virtues, the dangers,

owen a real friend helps us think our

, be our finest selves *anonymous* tell me

ho you are *french proverb* keep good com-

hem *scottish proverb* i have friends in over-

wap for the favor of the kings of the

lf is all important, because without

ne else in the world *eleanor roosevelt* life

love and be loved is the greatest

· P A L S ·

Words
F°R FRIENDS
T° LIVE BY

illustrated by Mary Engelbreit

**Andrews McMeel
Publishing**

Kansas City

www.andrewsmcmeel.com
www.maryengelbreit.com

 is a registered trademark of Mary Engelbreit Enterprises, Inc.

Words for friends to live by / illustrated by Mary Engelbreit.
    p. cm.
  ISBN 0-7407-1503-8
  1. Friendship--Quotations, maxims, etc. I. Engelbreit, Mary.

PN6084.F8 W65 2001
177'.62--dc21

                                            00-065021

01 02 03 04 05 MON 10 9 8 7 6 5 4 3 2 1

Illustrations by Mary Engelbreit
Design by Stephanie R. Farley

Contents

A few Words...
from
Mary Engelbreit

Dear Friends,

It's no surprise, I suppose, that friendship is at the heart of so many of my drawings. After all, good friends have always been central to my life.

I am a believer in old friends (though most of mine would prefer that I use the term "long-term" friends instead). In fact, many of my closest friends today were filling that same role 20, 30, some even 40 years ago. What a comfort such long-term relationships provide! For even though the years often lead us down diverging paths and sometimes pull us apart geographically, true friends are never really far from one another. When it really counts—when they are most needed or just wanted—true friends are always there, in spirit if not in person.

Friendship to me is forged over time but defined by moments. It's these moments that I try to capture in my art. Little girls make secret wishes while tossing coins into a stream, young brothers labor diligently to build a sandcastle on the beach, two grown friends share tea and quiet

conversation on a shady porch . . . nearly all of the images that find their way into my art are based on scenes that I've witnessed, and most of the people in them represent a close friend or family member. I believe that without friends to fill my life, I would have no life to fill my art.

I'm certainly not alone in finding inspiration in the thoughts and deeds of friends. Over the years, I've collected many quotes and writings about friendship—many of which say eloquently the very same things I try to communicate in my art. In this book I've combined many of these wonderful words on friendship with some of my own favorite drawings. It's my tribute to friends everywhere—especially my own dear friends. You know who you are . . . and I hope you know how very much you mean to me.

Your friend,

and the song, from beginning to end, I found in the heart of a friend *henry wadsworth longfellow* instinct teaches us to look for happiness outside of ourselves *blaise pascal* learn how to fall into friendship; but thou are in continue firm and constant *socrates* to like and dislike the same things, this is what makes a solid friendship *sallust* for a better, happier, more stable and civilized future, each of us must develop a sincere, warm-hearted feeling of brotherhood and sisterhood *dalai lama* what is a friend? a single soul dwelling in two bodies

...from great writers

Two lovely berries molded on one stem:
So, with two seeming bodies, but one heart.
–William Shakespeare

The growth
    of true friendship
may be a lifelong affair.
    —Sarah Orne Jewett

Be slow in choosing a friend, slower in changing.
    —Benjamin Franklin

Between loving friends
    there need be no secrets...
the trusting heart is always safe
    with another who truly cares!
        —Joan Walsh Anglund

When we can share—
that is the poetry
in the prose of life.
—Sigmund Freud

mary engelbreit

Friendship is the golden thread
that ties the heart of all the world.

–John Evelyn

Every man
passes his life
in search after friendship.
–Ralph Waldo Emerson

It is a sweet thing,
     friendship, a dear balm,
A happy and auspicious
          bird of calm.
                    —Shelbey Shelley

The language of friendship
     is not in words, but meanings.
               —Henry David Thoreau

A constant FRIEND is a thing rare and hard to find.
·Plutarch·

The proper office of a friend
is to side with you when you are wrong.
Nearly anybody will side with you
when you are right.
—Mark Twain

Good communication
is as stimulating as black coffee,
and just as hard to sleep after.

—Anne Morrow Lindbergh

Each friend represents a world in us,
a world possibly not born
until they arrive,
and it is only by this meeting
that a new world is born.
—Anaïs Nin

WE CANNOT TELL THE PRECISE MOMENT WHEN FRIENDSHIP IS FORMED. AS IN FILLING A VESSEL DROP BY DROP, THERE IS AT LAST A DROP WHICH MAKES IT RUN OVER; SO IN A SERIES OF KINDNESSES THERE IS AT LAST ONE WHICH MAKES THE HEART RUN OVER.

···· JAMES BOSWELL

It is hard to believe
that anything is worthwhile,
unless there is some eye
in common with our own,
some brief word uttered
now and then to imply
that what is infinitely precious to us
is precious alike to another mind.

—George Eliot

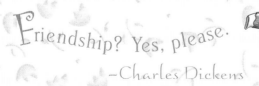

Friendship? Yes, please.

—Charles Dickens

One can never speak enough
of the virtues, the dangers,
the power of shared laughter.
    –Elizabeth Bowen

And the song,
    from beginning to end,
I found in the heart
    of a friend.
    –Henry Wadsworth Longfellow

Friendship
is the shadow
of the evening,
which strengthens
with the setting sun
of life.
–Jean de La Fontaine

Friendship's a noble name,
'tis love refined.
–Susanna Centlivre

25

be slow in choosing a friend, slower in changing benjamin franklin when we can share—that is the poetry in the prose of life sigmund freud friendship is the golden thread that ties the heart of all the world friendship's a noble name refined susann centlivre one can never speak enough of the virtues, the dangers, the power of shared laughter elizabeth bowen good communication is as stimulating as black coffee, and just as hard to sleep after anne morrow lindbergh friendship is the shadow of the evening, which strengthens with the setting sun

...from the sages and poets

A SMALL CIRCLE OF FRIENDS

Friendship is the bread of the heart.
—Mary Russel Mitford

What is a friend?
A single soul dwelling in two bodies.
—Aristotle

Instinct teaches us
to look for happiness
outside of ourselves.
–Blaise Pascal

Loyalty
is what we seek
in friendship.
–Cicero

What a thing friendship is—
World without end!
–Robert Browning

29

Be slow to fall into friendship;
but when thou are in,
continue firm and constant.
—Socrates

Small service is true service while it lasts;
Of humblest friends, bright creature!
Scorn not one: The daisy,
but the shadow that it casts,
Protects the lingering dewdrop
from the sun.
—William Wordsworth

And say my glory was I had such friends.
—William Butler Yeats

AH! HOW GOOD IT FEELS THE HAND of an OLD FRIEND · LONGFELLOW ·

To like and dislike the same things,
this is what makes a solid friendship.
—Sallust

Friendship is
a sheltering tree.

– Samuel Taylor Coleridge

The hearts
that never lean,
must fall.

– Emily Dickinson

For a better, happier, more stable and civilized future,
each of us must develop a sincere, warm-hearted feeling
of brotherhood and sisterhood.
—Dalai Lama

Friendship is Love without his wings!
—Lord Byron

My friends
are my estate.
—Emily Dickinson

I'D LIKE TO BE THE SORT of FRIEND THAT YOU HAVE BEEN TO ME
I'D LIKE TO BE THE HELP THAT YOU'VE BEEN ALWAYS GLAD TO BE;
I'D LIKE TO MEAN AS MUCH TO YOU EACH MINUTE OF THE DAY
AS YOU HAVE MEANT, OLD FRIEND of MINE, TO ME ALONG THE WAY
· EDGAR A. GUEST ·

The happiest moments my heart knows
are those in which it is pouring forth its affections
to a few esteemed characters.

—Thomas Jefferson

Learn to be silent
Let your quiet mind
listen and absorb.

—Pythagoras

Friendship consists in forgetting what one gives
and remembering what one receives.

—Dumas the Younger

Merry have we met and
Merry have we been,
Merry let us part and
Merry meet again!

*A*ll
that's dear
comes from
a friend.

—Horace

to have a good friend is one of the highest delights of life; to be a good friend is one of the noblest and most difficult *anonymous* on the road between *proverb* the houses of friends, grass does not grow *norwegian* friends are made by many acts *proverb* and lost by one *anonymous* a real friend helps us think our best thoughts, do our noblest deeds, be our finest selves *anonymous* tell me who you frequent and i'll tell you who you are *french proverb* keep good company and ye will be counted one of them

...from folk wisdom and word of mouth

THIS WAY

TO · THE
ENDS OF
THE
EARTH
10 KAJILLION·TRILLION ML

Precious gifts of friendship . . . knowing the heart of another,
sharing one's heart with another.

—Anonymous

Hold a true friend with both hands.

−Nigerian proverb

Friendship
   is the only cement
      that will ever hold
the world together.
   —author unknown

On the road
   between the homes of friends,
      grass does not grow.
         —Norwegian proverb

To have a good friend
   is one of the highest delights of life;
to be a good friend is one of the noblest
   and most difficult undertakings.
      —Anonymous

43

EVERYONE
NEEDS THEIR OWN
SPOT.

· ROBERT WHALEN ·

The fidelity of a dog
is a precious gift
demanding no less binding
moral responsibilities
than the friendship of
a human being.

—Anonymous

Our perfect companions
never have fewer than four feet.

—Anonymous

Tell me who you frequent
and I'll tell you who you are.
—French Proverb

Friends
are made
by many acts
and lost
by only one.
—author unknown

None is so rich as to throw away a friend.
—Turkish proverb

Keep Good Company and ye will be counted One of Them

·SCOTTISH·

There is no physician
like a new friend.
~author unknown

A TRUE FRIEND
IS THE
GREATEST OF
ALL BLESSINGS

Let us be the first
to give a friendly sign,
to nod first, smile first, speak first,
and—if such a thing is necessary—
forgive first.

—author unknown

A real friend helps us
think our best thoughts,
do our noblest deeds,
be our finest selves.

—author unknown

Time is not measured by clocks, but by moments.

GOSSIP

A hedge between keeps friendships green.

—French proverb

The best
mirror
is an
old friend.
—Anonymous

Be happy
with those
who are happy.
—Romans 12:15

I get by
with a little help
from my friends.
—John Lennon

two may talk together under the
same roof for many years, yet never
really meet; and two others at first
speech are old friends mary catherwood life
is fortified by many friendships to
love and be the greatest
hapiness of sydney smith the
hardest thing learning to
be a well of affection, and not a
fountain, to show them that we love
them, not when we feel like it, but
when they do nan fairbrother in the sweetness of friendship let there be
laughter and sharing of pleasures
are we not like the two

...from the witty
and the wise

We cherish our friends not for their ability to amuse us,
but for ours to amuse them.
—Evelyn Waugh

Two may talk together
under the same roof
for many years,
yet never really meet;
and two others at first speech
are old friends.
—Mary Catherwood

The best time
to make friends
is before you
need them.
—Ethel Barrymore

Friends are the
most important ingredient
in this recipe of life.
—Anonymous

It is one of the blessings of old friends
that you can afford to be stupid with them.
—Ralph Waldo Emerson

Life is fortified by many friendships—
To love and be loved
is the greatest happiness of existence.
—Sydney Smith

A faithful friend is a sturdy shelter;
who finds one finds a treasure.
—Sirach 6:14-15

THE MORE THE MERRIER

mary engelbreit

In reality,
we are still children.
We want to find
a playmate
for our thoughts
and feelings.
—Dr. Willhelm Stekel

There is no friend
like someone who has known you
since you were five.
—Anne Stevenson

Silences make the real conversations
between friends. Not the saying
but the never needing to say is what counts.
–Margaret Lee Runbeck

Accept what people offer.
Drink their milkshakes. Take their love.
—Wally Lamb

Live so that your friends can defend you,
but never have to.
—Ralph Waldo Emerson

Wear a smile
and have friends;
wear a frown
and have wrinkles.
—George Eliot

Old friends are the best.
King James used to call for his old shoes;
they were easiest on his feet.
—John Seldon

WHEN WE ARE GROWN WE'LL SMILE AND SAY
WE HAD NO CARES IN CHILDHOOD'S DAY—
BUT WE'LL BE WRONG. 'TWILL NOT BE TRUE.
I'VE THIS MUCH CARE.....I CARE FOR YOU.

Friend: one who knows all about you
and likes you just the same.
–Elbert Hubbard

the hand that reached out to me in fifth grade is still there *Susan Allen Toth* friends are God's way of taking care of us *anonymous* it is very easy to forgive others their... takes more grit and gu... ...rgive them for having w... ...own *Jessamyn West* i felt it shelter to speak to you *Emily Dickinson* thou wert my guide, philosopher, and friend *Alexander Pope* in each of my friends there is something that only some other friend can fully bring out *C. S. Lewis* best friend, my wellspring in the wilderness... what do we live for, if it is not to make lif...

...from friend
to friend

In the sweetness of friendship
let there be laughter and sharing of pleasures.
– Kahlil Gibran

Wherever
you are
it is your own
friends
who make
your world.
—William James

How rare and wonderful
is that flash of a moment
when we realize we have discovered a friend.
—William E. Rothschild

A cheerful friend
is like a sunny day
spreading sunshine all around.
—John Lubock

*R*einforce the stitch that ties us,
and I will do the same for you.

–Doris Schwerin

*A*re we not like the two volumes
of one book?

–Marceline Desbordes-Valmore

There is space within sisterhood
for likeness and difference, for the subtle differences
that challenge and delight;
there is space for disappointment—and surprise.

–Christine Downing

71

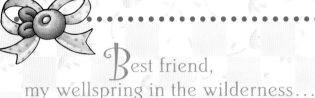

Best friend,
my wellspring in the wilderness…
What do we live for, if it is not to make life
less difficult for each other?
—George Eliot

The hand that reached out to me
in fifth grade is still there.

—Susan Allen Toth

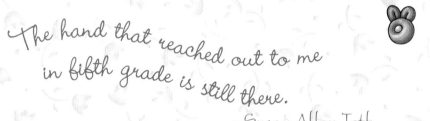

The depth of a friendship—
how much it means to us…
depends, at least in part,
on how many parts of ourselves
a friend sees, shares and validates.
—Lillian Rubin

In each of my friends
there is something that
only some other friend
can fully bring out.

–C. S. Lewis

Friends
are God's way
of taking care of us.

–Anonymous

mary engelbreit

A GIRL'S BEST FRIEND IS HER MOTHER

One is taught
by experience
to put a premium
on those few people
who can appreciate you
for what you are...
–Gail Godwin

I felt it shelter to speak to you.
–Emily Dickinson

It is very easy
to forgive others their mistakes;
it takes more grit and gumption
to forgive them for having witnessed your own.
–Jessamyn West

I suppose there is one friend
in the life of each of us
who seems not a separate person,
however dear and beloved,
but an expansion, an interpretation,
of one's self, the very meaning
of one's soul.
—Edith Wharton

Thou wert my guide, philosopher, and friend.

—Alexander Pope

EVER FORWARD, BUT SLOWLY.

VON BLÜCHER

here are three things that grow
more precious with age; old wood to
burn, old books to read, and old
friends to enjoy henry ford i always felt
that the great high privilege, relief
and comort of friendship was that
one had to   ing katherine mansfield i have fr   veralls whose
friendships i would not swap for the
favor of the kings of the world thomas
edison friendship with oneself is all
important, because without it one
cannot be friends with anyone else
in the world eleanor roosevelt plant a seed
of friendship; reap a boquet

...from the famous and familiar

friendship is a horizon,
which expands whenever we approach it.
—E. R. Hazlip

Books and friends
should be few
but good.
—Anonymous

There are three things
that grow more precious with age;
old wood to burn, old books to read,
and old friends to enjoy.
—Henry Ford

A true friend
is the best possession.
—Benjamin Franklin

I always felt that the great high privilege,
relief and comfort of friendship
was that one had to explain nothing.
–Katherine Mansfield

Friendship
is talking to your best friend
without words.

—Anonymous

There is nothing so great
   that I fear to do it for my friend;
nothing so small that I will disdain
   to do it for him.
                    —Sir Phillip Sidney

Constant use had not worn ragged
   the fabric of their friendship.
                    —Dorothy Parker

However deep our devotion may be to parents,
   or to children, it is our contemporaries alone
   with whom understanding is instinctive and entire.
                    —Vera Brittain

I have friends in overalls
whose friendships
I would not swap
for the favor of the kings
of the world.
–Thomas Edison

Walk beside me and be my friend.
–Albert Camus

You can date
the evolving life of the mind,
like the age of a tree,
by the rings of friendship
formed by the expanding central trunk.
–Mary McCarthy

But friendship is precious,
not only in the shade, but in the sunshine of life;
and thanks to a benevolent arrangement of things,
the greater part of life is sunshine.

—Thomas Jefferson

To me, fair friend, you never can be old, for as you were when first your eye I ey'd, such seems your beauty still.

Friendship is like a rose…
opening one petal at a time,
only as it unfolds…day by day
does it reveal its true beauty.
—Joan Walsh Anglund

Plant a seed of friendship;
reap a bouquet of happiness.
—Lois L. Kaufman

Friendship with oneself is all-important,
because without it one cannot be friends
with anyone else in the world.
—Eleanor Roosevelt

Oh, the comfort—the inexpressible comfort
of feeling safe with a person—having neither to
weigh thoughts nor measure words,
but pouring them all right out,
just as they are, chaff and grain together;
certain that a faithful hand will take and sift them,
keep what is worth keeping, and then with the
breath of kindness blow the rest away.

—Dinah Maria Mulock Craik

By friendship you mean the greatest love,
the greatest usefulness,
the most open communication,
the noblest sufferings,
the severest truth,
the heartiest counsel,
and the greatest union of minds
which brave men and women are capable.

—Jeremy Taylor

There are people
whom one loves
immediately and forever.
Even to know they are alive in
the world with one
is quite enough.

—Nancy Spain

...It is that my friends
have made the story of my life.
In a thousand ways they have turned my
limitations into privileges, and enabled me
to walk serene and happy in the shadow
cast by my deprivation.

–Helen Keller

Friendship improves happiness,
and abates misery,
by doubling our joy,
and dividing our grief.

–Joseph Addison

I have learned that to have a good friend
is the purest of all God's gifts,
for it is a love that has no exchange of payment.
—Frances Farmer

mary engelbreit

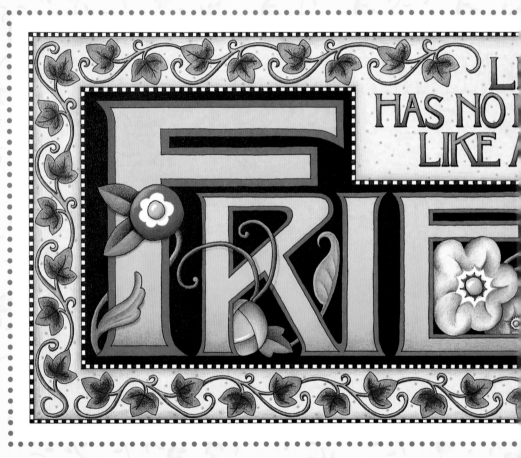

and the song, from beginning to en

wadsworth longfellow instinct teaches us to lo

blaise pascal be slow to fall into friends

firm and constant socrates to like and

makes a solid friendship sallust be sl

changing benjamin franklin when we can s

of life sigmund freud one can never speak

the power of shared laughter elizabeth

best thoughts, do our noblest deec

who you frequent and i'll tell you

pany and ye will be counted one of

alls whose friendships i would not

world thomas edison friendship with ones

it one cannot be friends with any

is fortified by many friendships